Bygone Holmesfield

Published by

Pynot
Publishing

Holmesfield • Derbyshire

First published in 2007 by Pynot Publishing and Holmesfield Village Society.

Copyright 2007 © Holmesfield Village Society

The author and Holmesfield Village Society wish to thank the following who have kindly allowed their photographs, postcards and archives to be made available to the village archives project:-

John Barber, Mary Beecroft, Linda Biggin, Joyce Biggin, Nev Biggin, the late Eric Booker, Connie Chandler, Kay Coxhead, Christine Eyre, Robert & Margaret Ford, Bob Gratton, Robert Green, Robin Greetham, Jean Helliwell, Christine Hibberd, Mary Keys, Mark Jowitt, Paul & Sylvia Meggitt, Pam & Ced Morris, Charles & Pat Morton, Derrick Paling, Tom Pearson, George Platts, Maurice Potts, Mark Ramsden, Roger Redfern, Mick Shufflebottom, Dan Taylor, Roger Webb, Barry Wheat, the late Florence Wheat, Alison & David Wilson, Graham & Cath Woollen.

ISBN 978-0-9552251-5-4

Pynot Publishing, 56 Main Road, Holmesfield, Dronfield, Derbyshire. S18 7WT
Tel: 0114 289 0348   Email: info@pynotpublishing.co.uk   www.pynotpublishing.co.uk

Front cover: A hand coloured postcard showing the centre of the village looking down Main Road towards Cowley Bar. The stone built cottages on the left have been mistakenly coloured as red brick, whilst the Travellers Rest seen by the junction with Cartledge Lane has since been substantially altered.

Rear cover: Also hand coloured, this postcard shows Cordwell Lane near Owler Bar and never ceases to amaze all but the oldest residents of the village when they see the little reservoir on the right. The waters have long since vanished as the area is now choked by Rhododendron bushes, but the the dam wall still survives as evidence of its former purpose.

Introduction

On behalf of Holmesfield Village Society, I would like to welcome you to this tour of our village in a bygone age and thank you for supporting us. By purchasing this album of largely Edwardian photographs you have helped raise funds for projects that will enhance Holmesfield for residents and visitors alike. The Millennium Garden and the newly refurbished village playground are just two examples of the tireless work put in by its members. New members are always welcome to join us.

The Holmesfield of 100 years ago was a totally different place to live in than it is today. It may be deemed to be fortunate in that it still retains some of its quiet byways, fabulous unspoilt views and largely stone built dwellings, but the make up of the village has changed forever as this once self-contained rural community in North Derbyshire inevitably evolves into a dormitory suburb of nearby Chesterfield and Sheffield like so many other villages in the area.

We can now only imagine life in Holmesfield as it was back then through faded photographs, dusty archives, and the memories of the ever dwindling number of village folk that can remember the days of old and the characters that were associated with it at one time or another.

No longer is it possible to buy provisions from the village shop, nor can pensions be collected from the post office. The village shop may no exist but people who prefer to buy pints of beer rather than pints of milk are still amply catered for as Holmesfield at least retains most of its public houses – a feature that still endears the village to some!

Since the Holmesfield Village Society began its archives project just a few short years ago, people have frequently requested a book of old photographs be published and we hope this first collection doesn't disappoint. We wish to publish other books on Holmesfield – not just just from a bygone age such as the one we present here, but also including more recent times. If you have any old photographs, documents or information that you feel would be of interest to the archives project, please get in touch. My thanks go to those listed opposite who have kindly loaned us such items, some of which you will now see before you.

Finally, people who wish to chat about the bygone times of Holmesfield are welcome to join the 'Memory Lane' group who meet on the first Tuesday of every month in the George & Dragon from 7.30pm.

Nick Wheat
Holmesfield
October 2007

Our album of photographs is presented as a journey around the village and our first view is of Cowley Bar, one of several hamlets that comprises the Parish of Holmesfield. Viewed from Kirk Farm with Kirk Villas just below on the right, the Rutland Arms is seen in the distance. A Frys chocolate sign is just visible but the building that it is attached to has long since disappeared along with the cottage in the middle distance that obscures the junction with Cowley Lane.

If we travel down the lane to Cowley, we eventually reach Cowley Mission which is kept in an excellent state of repair by its dedicated group of worshippers. Built in 1893, the Mission retains its close links with Cliff College in Calver. The surrounding area is much tidier these days than it appears to be in this rather rustic view.

Travelling up Main Road from Cowley Bar to Holmesfield we are presented with a scene that is arguably the least recognisable today. Only the sweep of the road is still present as the verge on the left is now punctuated by driveways to several houses and the hedge on the right has given way to a pleasant open green that runs in front of The Crescent.

Approaching the centre of the village we see this rare view of the Travellers Rest on the left and the Horns Inn on the right. Out of shot on the right is Rutland Cottage which we will see on the following pages. The hedgerow and tree on the right are destined to be swept away to make way for the village bus terminus which is still in use but no longer sees an hourly service to Dronfield and Sheffield.

Beyond the Travellers Rest is the junction with Cartledge Lane which takes the onward traveller to the Cordwell Valley via Millthorpe Lane. We will be travelling back this way later in our journey which for now continues towards Owler Bar.

Rutland Cottage was situated just below the Horns Inn. Here we see the original building in 1891 whereas the picture opposite shows its replacement in 1900. The last village shop was built on this site in the 1980s but had closed by the 1990s.

Eric Booker

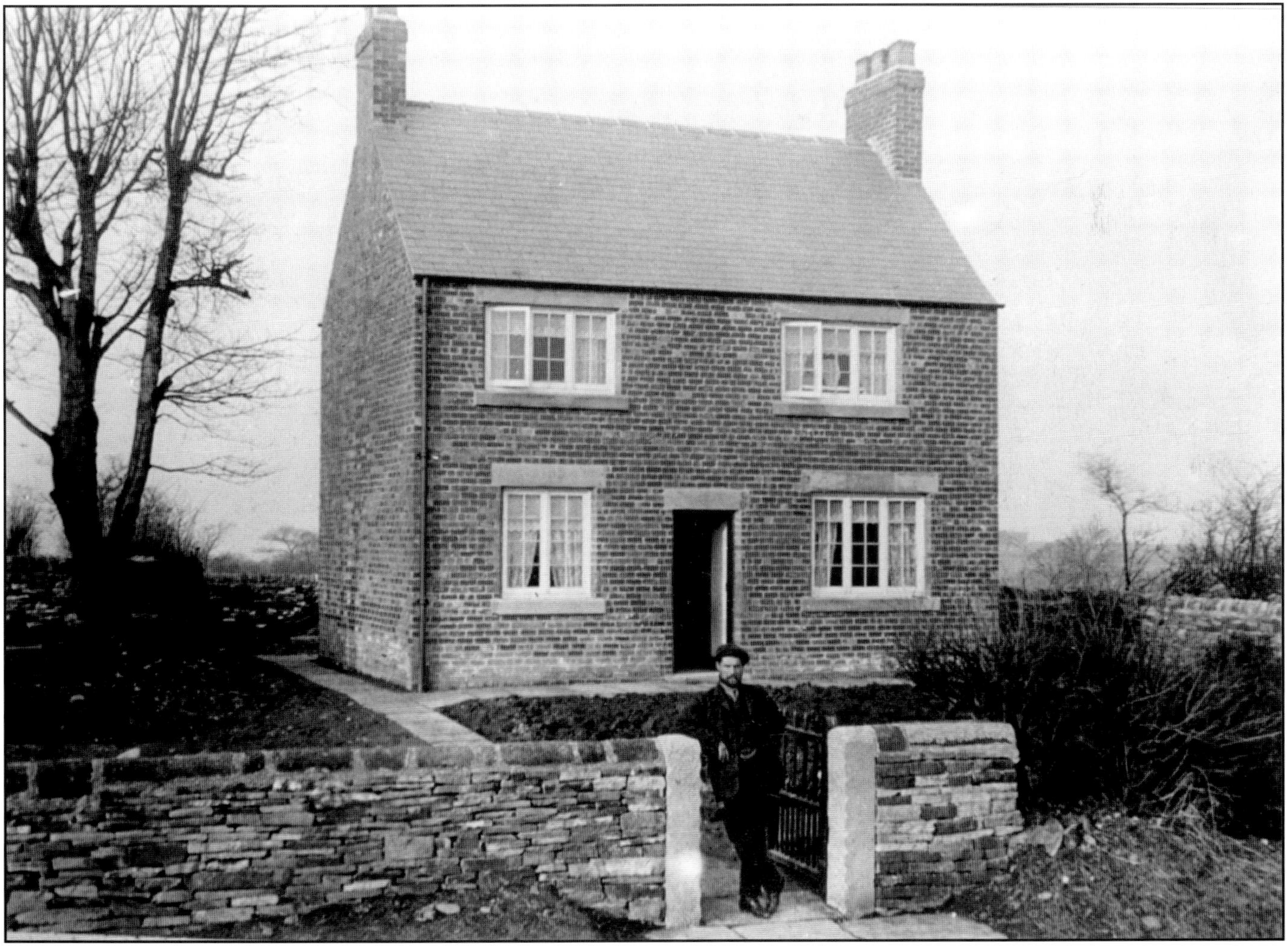

Rush Hour in Holmesfield c.1910! A similar view to our front cover image looking back towards Cowley Bar. One of the village smithys was located on the Green and is partially obscured by the telegraph pole. Only one of the children appears to be interested in the appearance of a cameraman on Main Road, the other two are seemingly more interested with what is coming up the hill, be it the horse and cart or the lady striding purposefully towards them.

The road junction with Cartledge Lane now has a telephone box within a triangle of grass in this undated view. The buildings seen here are within the Holmesfield Conservation Area and remain largely unaltered to this day. Trading appears to be far from brisk for Hadfields, Fruiterers of Barlow on the occasion the cameraman was back in the village.

Graham Woollen

Rev. Charles Bradshaw greets us on the steps of the Vicarage.

Graham Woollen

Rev. Charles Bradshaw – seen pictured with his wife – was the vicar of Holmesfield from 1887 to 1930 and was responsible for the addition of a chancel in 1895 to the church. Bradshaw was also responsible for the provision of a mission room in the Cordwell Valley which we will be seeing later.

The late Bessie Bunker[1], wrote that Mrs. Bradshaw was said to have been a lady of great charm and considerable musical ability. She was much in demand for social events and concerts held in the Sunday School during the winter months and for maypole dances performed by the Sunday School children under the tutorship of Miss Kathleen Bradshaw.

The Bradshaws moved away from the village upon Charles Bradshaw's retirement.

[1] Holmesfield Church of Saint Swithin – The Story of an Ancient Chapelry.

No. 8 Main Road is just up and across from the vicarage. It performed a variety of functions over the years as it was once a shop, post office, cobblers, smithy and even housed the village fire engine in its garage.

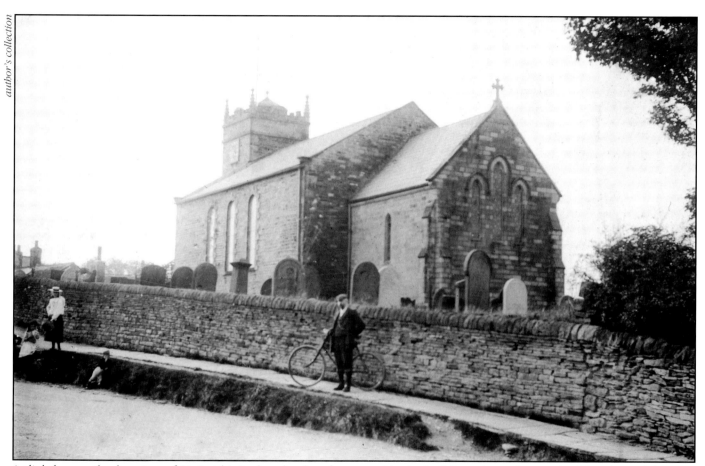

A slightly unorthodox view of St. Swithin's church taken from outside the building pictured opposite. The chancel that was added in 1895 is clearly shown and it was extended further in 1963 along with several other improvements to the church which included a porch, two new vestries and a kitchen.

Bob Gratton

The more traditional angle of Holmesfield St. Swithin's church and one that has adorned countless different postcards over the years. The tower and knave were built in 1826 to replace the original chapel that was said to have been in *'a ruinous state'*. The clock was originally installed in Norton church tower in 1818 and sold to Holmesfield in 1869. This view is possible once again following removal of a high conifer hedge that ran from the footpath to the church entrance.

A closer view of the church showing the original entrance before the porch was added in the 1960s as a memorial to the late Major W. & Mrs Wilson of Horsleygate Hall. This afforded further protection from the blustery winds that frequent this hill top location. A vestry was added to the rear of the bell tower which sadly lost its ornamental crown many years ago.

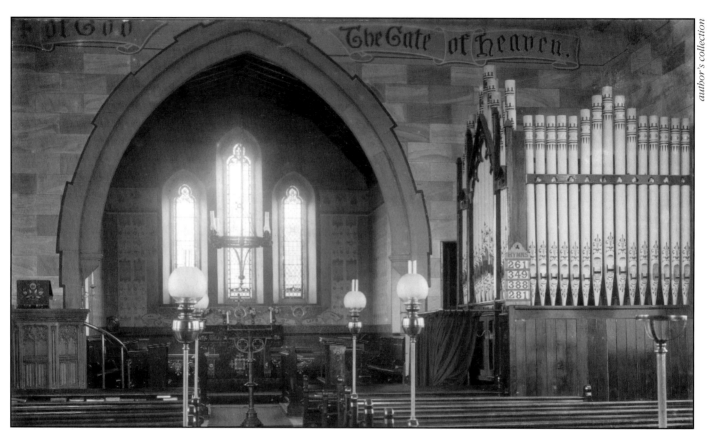

An evocative view of the interior of St. Swithin's church. Bessie Bunker noted that during the time of Rev. Bradshaw, the village schoolmaster, Mr Nichols, was also an outstanding church organist and choirmaster. This allowed time for practice and rehearsals for the choirboys and the boy soloists during school time. His protégé was John Smith of Lydgate who deputised during Nichols' holidays, playing the organ for all Services. A new organ was donated by Mrs. Rotherham Cecil of Dronfield in 1947 but even this is now defunct and seemingly beyond economic repair.

A later view showing how the beautiful stone walls had by now been painted over giving a starker appearance to the inside of the church. When the chancel was extended in 1963, a new East Window was installed as a memorial to Mr. & Mrs. J.T. Shepley of Woodthorpe Hall and can still be seen to this day.

Bob Gratton

One of the classic views of Holmesfield showing the church, village pond and one of its many public houses – the Angel Inn – which is seen in its original form before it was demolished and re-built in the late 1950s. The pond was unfortunately prone to being 'topped up' during rainy spells with various effluents from the adjacent Holmesfield Hall Farm and drinking from it was certainly not recommended, though it didn't deter village children from skating on it when it iced over!

This interesting aerial view of St. Swithin's church also shows the Angel Inn's reconstruction during 1956-7. The pub was re-built one half at a time and therefore never actually closed for the duration of the building works. Also seen in the bottom right is another of the village pubs, the George & Dragon. Postcards of the church are very common but cameramen never seemed to be inclined to cross the road and take the opposite view of the pub.

The peace and tranquillity of Edwardian Holmesfield as a couple promenade along the roadside towards the church. They would scarcely recognise Holmesfield Hall Farm today with its modern development of converted farm buildings.

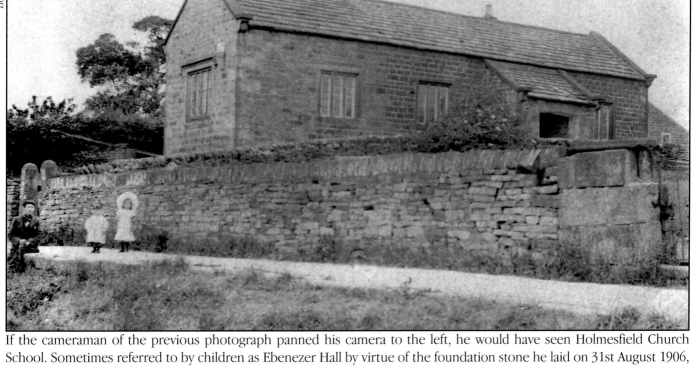

If the cameraman of the previous photograph panned his camera to the left, he would have seen Holmesfield Church School. Sometimes referred to by children as Ebenezer Hall by virtue of the foundation stone he laid on 31st August 1906, Hall was from Abbeydale Park and died on 28th June 1911 leaving a will that benefited many, including Holmesfield. He left money for the vicar and churchwardens to buy Government Stock *'sufficient to produce the yearly sum of £12 upon trust for the benefit of the poor inhabitants of the Chapelry of Holmesfield'*. It is interesting to note the porch which was later moved to the left side of the building as we view it. The Sunday School is still used by the 3rd Holmesfield Scouts, but for how much longer remains to be seen if a proposed church extension comes to fruition.

Travelling onwards towards Owler Bar, we drop down past Castle Hill, arriving at Holmesfield Common and the junction with Horsleygate Lane. A pinfold was located here (at the back of the wall behind the perambulator). The village school – Penny Acres – can be seen in the middle distance and is named after the ancient field on which it was built. The present 'new' school building was built in 1894-5 and still educates the village children up to 11 years of age. It is highly valued by parents and the local community. A Wesleyan chapel (out of picture) was situated down the lane on the left.

Unfortunately, we now have rather a jump in our journey as photographs and postcards of locations between Holmesfield and Owler Bar at the turn of the last century are extremely rare with just this solitary view of Lydgate coming to light so far. Despite all maps spelling this tiny hamlet 'Lidgate', all of the farms and houses are spelled 'Lydgate' regardless – a fact that even the Ordnance Survey have now finally come to accept – but as G.H.B. Ward once noted, the various places of the same name throughout the North are all pronounced the same – *'lidgett'*! The three cottages seem to be in a very dilapidated condition, but they survived until the 1950s when they were finally condemned. The far cottage – which is believed to have been a former nail makers – received the necessary remedial work to ensure it survived and was ultimately considerably extended. The road back to Holmesfield can be seen in the far distance curving up past Castle Hill.

The Robin Hood Inn pictured in the 1950s is situated at the top of a hill of the same name. It is now sadly closed – the only permanent pub closure within the Parish of Holmesfield so far – and has been extensively altered into housing, despite being substantial enlarged itself in the 1970s when it was still a thriving pub.

We'll now take a brief detour from Lydgate and travel to the end of Fanshawegate Lane with this view of Woodthorpe Hall in what appears to be a ruinous state. Just the front part of this once fine old Hall appears to be habitable, the remainder having a mixture of blocked off windows, broken windows and some windows that are missing altogether! The farm hand takes a break from his chores and poses for the camera with his fork, possibly before carrying on with delivering the milk we can see on the cart. The late Jack Shepley bought Woodthorpe Hall in the mid-1920s and oversaw its restoration into a much more fitting state of repair. It remains in the ownership of the Shepley family.

A group of motorcyclists pose for the camera outside the Peacock at Owler Bar c.1910. The pub stands high on the moors at the junction of five roads and has always been busy as a result. Peacock is a common name for a pub or hotel in this part of Derbyshire. There are or were Peacocks in Barlow (now the Old Pump), Cutthorpe, Baslow (now the Cavendish Hotel) and Bakewell and is a reference to the Duke of Rutland who owned much of the land as a Peacock sits atop the Duke's coat of arms. Until the second World War, live peacocks could be found in the pub grounds and were quite an attraction. This marks the end of the first part of our journey. From here we will travel back to Holmesfield via Cordwell and Millthorpe.

As we descend Horsleygate Road towards Millthorpe, the first point of interest is the small reservoir seen on the back cover of this book, before we come across a track that goes into Smeekley Wood (sometimes spelled Smeetly) on the right. The published postcard was incorrectly printed back to front and this view is seen as its correctly mirrored image.

The road now rises and the Barlow Hunt kennels built c.1879 are seen on the left. This view has changed little over the years other than the mode of transport for the hay.

The Barlow Hunt is synonymous with the Wilson family and especially Major W. Wilson of snuff fame. The family lived at Horsleygate Hall which is seen here in 1905 looking quite idyllic. The hall and its outbuildings look virtually the same today as they did here. Its wonderfully maintained gardens are a popular attraction when they are specially opened to the public.

No collection of photographs of Holmesfield in bygone days would be complete without one of the Barlow hounds and here we can see a hunt meeting in the field opposite Horsleygate Hall taken in 1920.

Taking a brief detour up Horsleygate Lane, we see this view of Middle Farm c.1910.

Bob Gratton

Postcards of Holmesfield Church are relatively common and so are ones of Eweford Bridge, but this scene is arguably the finest that has come to light so far. The buckets at the feet of the two ladies on the right will be filled with the clear water that emerges from a natural spring just behind the wall as the Children play around Millthorpe Brook. Unthank Lane goes off to the left and Fox Lane can be seen disappearing into the distance towards Ramsley Moor as the road we have travelled down curves round to the right. Eweford Bridge marks the point where Horsleygate Road becomes Cordwell Lane.

Travelling towards Unthank, we see Liversedge's tea rooms poking through a gap in the trees. The tea rooms were a very popular destination for visitors to Cordwell Valley.

A delightful photograph taken from near Unthank Lane Farm as a group of visitors in their Sunday best take in the clean air of a pastoral Cordwell Valley. The hamlet of Cordwell is left behind them as Holmesfield Church on the horizon oversees the proceedings.

The provision of a Church Mission Room in the Cordwell Valley was another of Rev. Charles Bradshaw's achievements. This was built for the benefit of those that found the uphill trek to worship in St. Swithin's church too arduous a task. The building lasted for many years and was not demolished until c.1970.

Sheep dipping was done in Millthorpe Brook and this scene is believed to be near the weir at Cordwell.

The farmhouse of Cordwell Farm is seen from Cordwell Lane peering behind the tree. Horse mounting steps can be seen on the grass verge as two young boys stare intently at the cameraman.

The victorian writer, Edward Carpenter, was the most famous former resident of Millthorpe and he lived in this cottage with its orchard and market garden from 1883 until 1922, attracting the great literary luminaries of the day to visit. Sandal making was another cottage industry that supplemented his income from writing. This is the view of what has now become Carpenter House from the footpath that runs from Unthank to Millthorpe. Carpenter died in Guildford in 1929.

The Royal Oak re-opened in 2005 following over a year of closure and has become the focal point of Millthorpe again. Here we see the tranquillity of old Millthorpe at its best in this famous photograph that shows Harriett Haslam and her daughter Kate Webster who was to follow in her mother's footsteps as landlady.

Just beyond the Royal Oak we come to a crossroads. Seen from the foot of Millthorpe Lane which takes us back to Holmesfield, Cordwell Lane (which we have just travelled along) is to the right, Mill Lane is straight ahead taking us down to the ford and New Road is on the left which takes us to Barlow and onwards towards Chesterfield. Just out of shot on the left was a thatched tea room.

The ford at Millthorpe is situated across from the old water mill and has changed little since this picture taken c.1910. Visitors have always been attracted to this feature of Cordwell Valley and it is still enjoyed by walkers and horse riders alike.

Down Mill Lane we see what was destined to become an act of sheer vandalism. This fine old water mill closed not long after the Second World War and was abandoned. When it was bought by a builder it was slowly stripped of all its re-usable building materials and ultimately demolished despite being afforded Grade II listed status. The lack of action by the local authority was disgraceful and Millthorpe lost forever one of its most charming features.

Graham Woollen

This rare photograph shows the rear of the mill and the mill stream that fed the water wheel. The young lady holding the small child is believed to be Ivy Helliwell. Ivy was a keen observer of village events and kept a diary almost until she died in 1988. She formerly lived in Bank Green Cottage off Fox Lane but had to leave it in the mid-1950s. This allowed a once charming property to sadly go to rack and ruin.

Travelling back towards Holmesfield along Millthorpe Lane we pass Chatsworth Cottages about half way up. Several postcards have been produced showing the front of them, but not so many show something of the view of Cordwell Valley they enjoy.

At the top of Millthorpe Lane, the road turns sharply left and becomes Cartledge Lane, travelling on towards Holmesfield. If we turn right we see Cartledge Hall, the one time residence of celebrated author Robert Murray Gilchrist.

Next door to Cartledge Hall is the magnificently imposing Cartledge Grange which is one of the most spectacular old houses in Holmesfield.

Bob Gratton